Polly Waterfield and Timothy K...

GYPSY Jazz

Songs and dances from across Europe for violin with piano
Chants et danses d'Europe pour violon avec piano
Lieder und Tänze aus ganz Europa für Violine mit Klavierbegleitung

© 1996 by Faber Music Ltd
First published in 1996 by Faber Music Ltd
3 Queen Square London WC1N 3AU
Cover design by Lynette Williamson
Music processed by Wessex Music Services
Printed in England by Halstan and Co Ltd
All rights reserved

ISBN 0 571 51637 8

FABER ff MUSIC

Introduction

Gypsy Jazz is an invitation to a musical journey! It gives elementary players an opportunity to travel horizons beyond 'classical' music and there discover a world of traditional songs and dances. You can wind your way through the exotic musical landscape of Eastern Europe, or stumble upon more familiar territory with a Celtic lilt, or explore contemporary pieces inspired by folk and jazz. We have chosen a variety of keys, metres and tempi to make the journey enticing to the pupil and useful to the teacher; the pieces appear roughly in order of difficulty. We hope they will also be enjoyed by the older learner as a technically undemanding exploration into different musical worlds. Many of the tunes can stand on their own without accompaniment, but the piano part adds zest and character.

Happy travelling!

Polly Waterfield and Timothy Kraemer 1996

Introduction

Gypsy Jazz vous invite à un voyage musical! Ce recueil offre aux interprètes débutants l'occasion d'explorer des domaines autres que celui de la musique dite 'classique' pour découvrir l'univers des danses et des chants traditionnels. Vous pourrez flâner dans les contrées musicales exotiques de l' Europe orientale, fréquenter des lieux plus familiers grâce à un rythme celtique, ou encore étudier des pièces contemporaines inspirées du folk et du jazz. Nous avons choisi une gamme de tons, de mètres et de tempos qui devrait séduire l'exécutant et intéresser l'enseignant; d'une manière générale, les pièces sont rangées par degré de difficulté. Nous espérons que ce recueil offrira aussi à l'interprète plus confirmé un moyen techniquement simple d'explorer un univers musical nouveau. Plusieurs des mélodies peuvent très bien être exécutées sans accompagnement mais la partie de piano leur donne sans doute plus de caractère.

Bon voyage!

Polly Waterfield et Timothy Kraemer 1996

Einleitung

Gypsy Jazz lädt den Spieler zu einer musikalischen Reise ein und eröffnet Anfängern die Möglichkeit, eine Welt jenseits der 'klassischen' Werke zu entdecken, wo sie die ganze Vielfalt volkstümlicher Lieder und Tänze kennenlernen können. Ausgehend von den fremdartigen Klängen Osteuropas kann man vertrauteres Terrain bei einer keltischen Weise entdecken, oder zeitgenössische Stücke ausprobieren, die von Jazz- und Folk-Elementen beeinflußt sind. Wir haben verschiedene Tonarten, Taktarten und Tempi gewählt, um die musikalische Reise für den Schüler reizvoll und gleichzeitig instruktiv zu gestalten; die Stücke sind in etwa nach ihrer Schwierigkeit geordnet. Wir hoffen, daß auch ein älterer Anfänger an den Stücken Freude findet, da sie ihm ohne allzugroße technische Hürden verschiedene musikalische Welten aufschließen.Viele der Weisen können ohne Begleitung musiziert werden, die Klavierstimme macht das Ganze aber schwungvoller und runder.

Gute Reise!

Polly Waterfield und Timothy Kraemer 1996

Chailean's cows
(a cowherd's love-song)

das Liebeslied eines Kuhhirten   Le chant d'amour du vacher

Scottish traditional
arr. P. W.

This music is copyright. Photocopying is illegal.

Elenke

Bulgarian traditional
arr. P. W.

The words of the song tell this story: Elenke is called to her lover's sick-bed but she refuses to go: "I won't leave this merry dancing for a moment. Dancing makes me happy!"

Im zugrundeliegenden Liedtext wird die folgende Geschichte berichtet: Elenke wird an das Krankenbett ihres Liebsten geholt, will aber nicht gehen: "Ich werde diese fröhliche Tanzveranstaltung keinen Augenblick verlassen, Tanzen macht mich glücklich!"

Voici ce dont traite le chant: Elenke est appelée au chevet de son amant malade mais elle refuse de s'y rendre: "Je ne quitterai pas une seconde ce bal si joyeux. J'ai tant de plaisir à danser!"

Cuckoo

Russian folksong
arr. T. K.

Moderato (♩ = 115)

Through my window

An meinem Fenster   Par ma fenêtre

Hungarian tune
arr. T. K.

The abandoned maiden bemoans her fate, looking through her window at the moon.
Das verlassene Mädchen steht am Fenster, sieht den Mond an und bedauert sein Schicksal.
Une jeune fille abandonnée déplore sa triste destinée tout en observant la lune par sa fenêtre.

Kalamatianos

Greek traditional
arr. P. W.

* **Fine** last time
* **Fine** *beim letzten Mal*
* **Fine** la dernière fois

Lazy time

Zeit des Faulenzens   Paresse

Timothy Kraemer

Hassapikos

Greek traditional
arr. P. W.

This is a traditional dance tune which would have been used by Greek butchers on their festival days.
Dies ist ein traditioneller Tanz griechischer Metzger zu ihren Festtagen.
Il s'agit ici d'un air de danse traditionnel que les bouchers grecs utilisaient le jour de leur festival.

Through the rainbow

Hinter dem Regenbogen   A travers l'arc-en-ciel

Polly Waterfield

Old Czech folk tune

Alte tschechische Volksweise   Vieille mélodie populaire tchèque

arr. T. K.

Carolan's Farewell

Carolans Abschied   L'Adieu de Carolan

Turlough Carolan
arr. P. W.

* imitate a harp
* *Wie eine Harfe*
* imiter une harpe

Carolan was a blind Irish harpist of the eighteenth century, and the story goes that he wrote this tune on his death-bed.
Carolan war im 18. Jahrhundert ein blinder Hafenspieler in Irland. Das Lied hat er angeblich auf seinem Sterbebett geschrieben.
Carolan, harpiste irlandais aveugle du dix-huitième siècle, aurait écrit cette mélodie sur son lit de mort.

Greek song and dance

Griechisches Lied und griechischer Tanz   Chant et danse grecs

Timothy Kraemer